Before the Bell:
30 Days of Devotions for Teachers

Jennie G. Scott

All rights reserved. No part of this book may be reproduced in any form or by any electronic or mechanical means, including information storage and retrieval systems, without written permission from the author, except in the case of a reviewer, who may quote brief passages embodied in critical articles or in a review. Trademarked names appear throughout this book. Rather than use a trademark symbol with every occurrence of a trademarked name, names are used in an editorial fashion, with no intention of infringement of the respective owner's trademark. The information in this book is distributed on an "as is" basis, without warranty. Although every precaution has been taken in the preparation of this work, neither the author nor the publisher shall have any liability to any person or entity with respect to any loss or damage caused or alleged to be caused directly or indirectly by the information contained in this book.

Table of Contents

Day 1 - A Noticeably Different Environment
Day 2 - A Great Calling, but Small Beginnings
Day 3 - A Malleable Mindset for Maximum Impact
Day 4 - A Whisper at a Time
Day 5 - An Eternal Perspective
Day 6 - Choose to Trust the Seeds
Day 7 - Each Child is a Miracle
Day 8 - Equipped to Meet the Demands
Day 9 - Ever-Evolving Tasks
Day 10 - Flesh Defeated By the Spirit
Day 11 - Getting Past a One-Dimensional View
Day 12 - He Reaches Down in Compassion
Day 13 - In Alignment with Your Assignment
Day 14 - It's Not About Me
Day 15 - Learning What Makes Them Tick
Day 16 - More Than What Vision Reveals
Day 17 - Negativity Breeds Negativity
Day 18 - Renewed in His Presence
Day 19 - The Good in What He Allows
Day 20 - The Inevitability of Hard Times
Day 21 - The Marathon of the Classroom
Day 22 - The Words They Remember

Day 23 - Understanding the Seasons
Day 24 - We Are Acting on Behalf of God
Day 25 - We Teach Them How to Navigate the World
Day 26 - What I Need and What I Want
Day 27 - What It's Like to Be Loved
Day 28 - What to Do When You Need Guidance
Day 29 - What We Accept and What We Condone
Day 30 - When Truths Come to Light

Dedication

Teachers - you are my people. Every day, you do the impossible with far too many resources and far too little respect. No one does more important work than you do. You change the lives of children and you dramatically impact the culture of this country. Thank you for your dedication to excellence.

Day 1 - A Noticeably Different Environment

"Pray then like this: "Our Father in heaven, hallowed be your name. Your kingdom come, your will be done, on earth as it is in heaven. Give us this day our daily bread, and forgive us our debts, as we also have forgiven our debtors. And lead us not into temptation, but deliver us from evil." Matthew 6: 9-13

When was the last time you begged God to make your classroom a place full of his presence? I think subconsciously we all want His kingdom to come into our rooms, and to some extent we work to make it a reality. But have we ever truly asked?

Do we ever really beg God to bring the fullness of who He is into a world desperately void of His peace?

For many of the children we teach, they have no understanding of who God is, and they have not been taught what His presence can do. In a school, you can't stand before them and preach a sermon, but you can facilitate an environment where God's presence dwells. And where God is, people take notice. Your children may not be able to explain what's different in your room, but they will be able to perceive that there is a difference. They will feel safe and loved, and peace will reign where they're accustomed to chaos. They will notice, and God can begin a softening of their hearts that paves the way for eventual surrender.

Lord, I am desperate for my classroom to be a place that is noticeably different in the chaos of my children's lives. I beg you to fill my classroom with your Holy presence and to enter into the hearts that don't know you. Let me do everything in my power to create peace, calm, security, and love. I pray there will be a noticeable difference when my students cross the threshold into my room. Each day, Lord, be noticeable in our environment. Be present in our conversations. Be sovereign in our lives.

Day 2 - A Great Calling, but Small Beginnings

"For whoever has despised the day of small things shall rejoice, and shall see the plumb line in the hand of Zerubbabel." Zechariah 4:10

He came into my classroom a tough-looking teenager. I had seen his permanent record, seen his earlier scores. The 14 year old had the reading ability of a second grader, and I was at a loss. Secondary trained, I was proficient in teaching Shakespeare. I could teach diagramming sentences all day long, and I had no problem instructing on argument support. Teaching reading, though? Where could I even begin?

After doing some research and talking to other teachers, I developed a game plan. The media specialist loaned me some audio books, and I differentiated his assignments. We worked on simple sight words, and though it wasn't immediate, we made progress. But it was slow, and it was small.

I was frustrated. I knew the expectation for students leaving my class, and I knew he wouldn't meet them. There was no way to make up seven grade levels in the course of a semester, and I was afraid of how it would look.

Really, I was afraid of how I would look.

Sure enough, by the end of the semester, he made improvements. Testing showed his reading improved by a grade level. It was small, but it was something.

Isn't that how life is, though? We want grand, immediate changes to happen in the course of a few days, and we get frustrated when the changes take time. We see the small changes, but to us they're just small.

Yet God reminds us that small is something. Small beginnings make room for great changes, and without them, we remain the same.

This year, small beginnings will take place in your room, and with many of them, you will never see the ultimate result. But do not despise them. Your calling is great though it may feel small. Your small obedience paves the way for great changes to come.

Father, it can be agonizing to work so hard and see so little change. It can be discouraging and frustrating to see such smallness when I desire great change. But help me remember that there's so much hidden from what I see, and you are trustworthy with it all. Small is something, and I choose to trust you with it.

Day 3 - A Malleable Mindset for Maximum Impact

"Having gifts that differ according to the grace given to us, let us use them: if prophecy, in proportion to our faith; if service, in our serving; the one who teaches, in his teaching; the one who exhorts, in his exhortation; the one who contributes, in generosity; the one who leads, with zeal; the one who does acts of mercy, with cheerfulness." Romans 12:6-8

Boy, can we teachers get stuck in our ways.

We often teach the way we were taught, and once we've taught a lesson with relative success, we file it away and repeat it again and again. But what we need to remember is that what worked once isn't the only way, and the way we learned isn't the way for everyone.

Scripture says, "If you are a teacher, teach well." I'm not sure about your experience, but in mine, teaching well is tough. It's trial and error, learning new methods, venturing into uncharted waters. Teaching well is a combination of learning from others and trusting your gut. Teaching well looks different your second year versus your twentieth, and teaching well looks different first period than it does fifth.

The hardest part of teaching well is that it means students must learn well, too.
Are you the kind of teacher who does whatever it takes? Are you willing to think outside your box, incorporate new methods? Teaching well requires a malleable mindset. Is this what you have?

Lord, I really do want to teach well. I want the hours I spend preparing and teaching to make an impact, and I want my students to learn from my lessons. Sometimes the easy way out is to do what I've always done. Be my strength, God, when I want my weakness to reign. Give me the determination to teach well and not just teach. Remind me what's at stake.

Day 4 - A Whisper at a Time

"And your ears shall hear a word behind you, saying, "This is the way, walk in it," when you turn to the right or when you turn to the left." Isaiah 30:21

Even with my back turned, I recognized the voice. The students were not supposed to be talking, but this child couldn't help herself. She was a social butterfly, and she struggled with self-control. Her voice floated up to my ears, and I knew exactly who it was.

When we are children of God, we begin to recognize and hear his voice regardless of where we are. His Holy Spirit convicts us, and He also guides us when we're seeking direction.

In the classroom, we need direction daily. We need to know how to manage our tasks and how to approach each child. God promises to be the voice behind us offering direction. But He will not yell or take over uninvited. We must first ask.

When the job confuses you, ask for direction. When students confound you, ask for direction. When pressures constrict you, ask for direction.

He will whisper, one step at a time, "This is the way. Walk in it."

Jesus, so often I strike out on my own, confident in my abilities and ready to blaze a trail. But so often I get in the middle of the path I've chosen and feel confused, wandering and aimless. I don't know what to do next or where to turn. Show me, God. Slow me down and guide me one step at a time. Give me ears to discern your voice and a heart to obey it. Remind me that you are the source of omniscient power, and I am to follow you.

Day 5 - An Eternal Perspective

"So God created man in his own image, in the image of God he created him; male and female he created them." Genesis 1:27

You have students who annoy you, don't you? For whatever reason, there are children who tap dance on your last nerve, and the sight of them walking down the hall fills you with dread. They know just how to push your buttons, and though you feel guilty, you secretly hope they'll be absent.

I know. I've been there.

When we find ourselves thinking we'd rather not be with the students we've been given, it's time for a reset. It's time to re-remember what we so easily forget, which is that each child whose face looks to us is an image-bearer of our God. Each little person who fills our rooms was created lovingly and painstakingly just the way he is and just as we were, too.

Their habits that annoy you and behaviors that irritate you are a part of who they are, but they are not the most important part. The core truth that they bear the image of God is what matters most, and we need to remind ourselves daily of this fact.

Change your mentality, and you'll change your outlook.

God, I need you to give me your eyes for these children. From my human perspective, I see the flaws and shortcomings, and these overwhelm my thoughts for my students. Exchange my judgmental and limited sight for your eternal and all-loving perspective. Every morning, help me remember that you created each child on purpose and just as they are to accomplish your purposes. They were not created to be students who act as I wish, but they were made to bring your glory to the earth. Teach me to see them like you do.

Day 6 - Choose to Trust the Seeds

"Therefore, my beloved brothers, be steadfast, immovable, always abounding in the work of the Lord, knowing that in the Lord your labor is not in vain." 1 Corinthians 15:58

I threw my bag into the passenger's seat and slammed the car door. The day was finally over, and I was free to go. My thoughts kept circling back to 4th period and the lack of progress I was making with them. I had tried everything I knew to teach the material. My lessons were thorough and included every multiple intelligence, but they just weren't working. My kids weren't getting it, and all I was getting was frustrated. It felt like everything I was doing was in vain. A waste of time. A failure.

We teachers have grandiose plans of seeing immediate growth in a short period of time. We see invisible light bulbs above our students' heads, and we picture them glowing with understanding. We think that if we just work hard enough and plan the right things, all students will learn and they will all succeed.

That's not reality.

But when we are working in the ways of the Lord, we can trust that despite what we see, we are not working in vain. At the right time, fruit will produce. It may not be during our academic year, and we may not even see it. But the harvest will come. God cannot go against his word, and his word says our labor is not in vain. When it feels like it is, we must choose to trust him.

Lord, I feel like I'm failing. I'm doing everything I know to do and working as hard as I can, but there is a disconnect. My emotions and senses tell me I'm working in vain, but I am choosing to believe you instead. I'm choosing to trust that the seeds I plant now will produce a great harvest in your perfect timing. When I'm frustrated, calm me. When I'm discouraged, change my mindset. When I think it's all in vain, remind me that it's not.

Day 7 - Each Child is a Miracle

"But Moses said to God, 'Who am I that I should go to Pharaoh and bring the children of Israel out of Egypt?'" Exodus 3: 11

When my son, my first child, was born, I remember looking at him in disbelief. Swaddled in my arms was God's love made tangible, and I could not get over the miracle that he was.

Each child in your classroom is a miracle, too.

In the day to day grind of lessons to teach and behavior to manage, we often lose sight of exactly what has been entrusted to us. We have the great blessing and enormous responsibility of caring for and shepherding miracles. Your students' parents have given you what matters most in their lives - their children. Each day, they release their babies into the safety of your classroom, and they believe time spent with you is what will make their children thrive.

Never lose sight of what you are allowed to do. Never stop asking, "Who am I, Lord, that I should be trusted like this?" Never take for granted that you are granted the greatest privilege any parent could give.

God, humble me today and allow me to understand the magnitude of the calling on my life. I am not just a teacher. I am a caretaker and shepherd of the greatest miracles you give. Allow me to see through Spirit-led eyes and give me your thoughts for these children. Help me to love each child unconditionally and treat each child as if he were my own. Fill me to overflowing with your love.

Day 8 - Equipped to Meet the Demands

"Everyone to whom much was given, of him much will be required, and from him to whom they entrusted much, they will demand the more." Luke 12: 48

Some days it feels like too much is demanded of us, and most of the time, we feel that what is asked of us is simply impossible. We are expected to be everything to everyone and to do it all perfectly.

It is overwhelming.

But when we look at why so much is demanded and asked of us, things change. Much is demanded *because we have been given much*. Much is asked *because we have been entrusted with much*.

The pressures we feel are a direct result of our blessings. In addition to that, the demands we must meet flow from what we have been given. We are equipped to meet every demand and to answer what is asked - if we look to the correct source.

God has already made available what we need, and He is faithful to reveal it if we go to him.

Our trouble comes when we try to do it on our own.

Lord, how foolish I am. When I feel the overwhelming demands of teaching, my first response is to feel helpless or to complain. When these times come, turn my eyes to you. Bring my heart back to the source of all I need. You, God, have made a way for me. You, God, give just what I need. You, God, are the answer to my hardships. Help me remember that have blessed me immeasurably and that nothing I do is separate from your gifts.

Day 9 - Ever-Evolving Tasks

"But Jesus looked at them and said, "With man this is impossible, but with God all things are possible." Matthew 19:26

Today at the grocery store, I ran into a teacher friend who is now retired. We caught up on her grandchildren and new pursuits, and we talked about where education is headed. We talked about the standards and testing, the stresses that teachers face. We admitted that the changes over the years are seeming more and more impossible, and the job seems harder and harder.

The task teachers face every day is always evolving, and with every change comes a new challenge. Many teachers feel they just don't have what it takes to do the job well anymore.

But Jesus tells us that nothing is impossible - with God. On our own, we certainly don't have what it takes. But with the guidance and strength from the One who made us, we can do all things.

Every day, remind yourself that you are not alone in the job you're asked to do. You have the source of all wisdom available to you at every moment. He is faithful to answer your prayers, and He is faithful to guide your paths.

God, I'm choosing to believe your truth that "with God all things are possible." This is true regardless of my circumstances, and because you have declared it, I will believe it. Take away my pessimistic attitude that wants to give up, and replace it with the assurance that with you, I can do all things.

Day 10 - Flesh Defeated By the Spirit

"But the fruit of the Spirit is love, joy, peace, patience, kindness, goodness, faithfulness, gentleness, self-control; against such things there is no law."
Galatians 5: 22-23

I had to step outside my classroom to regain my composure. All semester, this class had been collectively uncooperative, trying my patience and my faith. I had tried so hard to be kind and understanding, but my resolve was wearing thin. Another display of disrespect shocked me greatly, and rather than react in my flesh, I walked my flesh into the hall. I would not let a 14 year old undo me.

After several deep breaths and a desperate "Help me Jesus" prayer, I stepped back into the room ready to move ahead.

Teaching can try you, can't it? Spending all day with children who have been raised with different values and who are asserting their independence can test your patience in unbelievable ways. You want to react with a Christlike attitude, but in heated moments, your resolve begins to crumble and your sin nature wants to show out!

The only way to remain Christlike in the most trying circumstances is to be controlled by the Holy Spirit. It is to deny your flesh and react from a supernatural place, a place you naturally will not visit. Christ in you can do what no amount of effort on your own ever can.

You will probably face a hard situation today where your emotions will threaten to take over. Pray now for the fruits of the Spirit to come through instead.

Father, when I am faced with hardships, my sinful self is always at the surface of my reactions, threatening to show itself. I'm asking that your Holy Spirit will rise in me instead, reigning victorious. Show yourself mighty through me, and help me show love to those I encounter. Let my flesh be defeated by the power of your Spirit.

Day 11 - Getting Past a One-Dimensional View

"Trust in the Lord with all your heart, and do not lean on your own understanding."
Proverbs 3:5

It was my first year teaching. Barely 21 and as a green as they come, I was given the 7th graders who were, shall we say, not the top of the class. The students filling the desks that year were seasoned in teacher-torture, and they were quite proficient. Academic work was the last thing on their minds, and nothing in my teacher-training prepared me for what to do. I had spent hours making my classroom vibrant and planning our get-to-know-you activities. I carefully created the handouts to distribute, and I agonized over which novels to teach. I did everything in my power to start the school year well. And it bombed.

They looked at me like I was insane. They laughed at the activities we did. They refused to take notes, and sitting still was a laughable suggestion. I was devastated and defeated by the end of week one.

Leaning on my own understanding was all I knew to do. I was a teacher, at last, and so I assumed I could figure it out. I never did. Trial and error just became error after error, and regardless of what I did, it was never the right choice. I cried almost every day, and I knew I had made a terrible choice.

What I never did, I'm ashamed to say, was ask the Lord for his wisdom with those children. Many of them had serious issues beyond the academics, but I naively believed those weren't my concern. If I had stepped out of my teacher-brain and looked at them with a loving heart, perhaps I could have made some progress. But I didn't. I didn't ask God to reveal what I needed to know, and as a result, my own understanding was never enough.

I wish I could find those children today and apologize to them. I had been taught to see them as students, but I failed to treat them as people.

Ask God today to give you his understanding. I promise your own will never be enough.

God, we teachers are so limited. We have a one-dimensional view of our students, and we often miss the most important parts. We desperately need your understanding of the people filling our rooms. Help us to consider each child carefully, looking beyond the obvious and seeing their hearts. Show us what we can never see on our own, and help us rely on you more than ourselves.

Day 12 - He Reaches Down in Compassion

"As a father shows compassion to his children, so the Lord shows compassion to those who fear him. For he knows our frame; he remembers that we are dust."
Psalm 103: 13-14

The bell rang, signaling that the class period was finally over. My students rushed out, heading to their next class, and I collapsed into my chair, thankful to have a break.

Nothing had gone the way I planned. No one seemed to learn what I tried so desperately to teach. There was nothing else to call it - the class was a colossal failure.

Perhaps I was, too.

I dropped my eyes to the desk covered in papers and post-its, and the tears sprang to my eyes uninvited. "I can't do this," I thought. "I don't have what it takes."

Have you ever felt the same way? Have you looked at the needs in your classroom and realized just how overwhelming your job is?

When moments like these happen, don't become so discouraged you give up. Become so desperate you seek God. In every place we are weak, He is strong. He knows our weaknesses and does not disqualify us because of them. He reaches towards us, tender and compassionate. He speaks into us, whispering truth and grace. He invites us to rest in Him, relinquishing it all.

Decide today that your weaknesses point to your great need for a Savior, and that when you realize your failures, you'll resolve to lean into Him even more.

Father, thank you for being all that we are not. Remind us that you are ever-present, even in our struggles, and that you desire to extend your compassion to the hurting places in our hearts. Be our strength. Be our teacher. Be our way.

Day 13 - In Alignment with Your Assignment

"But they who wait for the Lord shall renew their strength; they shall mount up with wings like eagles; they shall run and not be weary; they shall walk and not faint." Isaiah 40: 31

I know you're tired. There's no tired like teacher-tired, and there's no relief except summer vacation. Perpetual exhaustion is part of this profession, and some days you feel like you will barely make it.

You will.

There will always be just 24 hours in a day, and you probably can't take multiple days off to sleep until you're rested. But what you can do is ask for supernatural rest. Take your exhaustion to the Lord and confide how you feel. Ask him to deliver you from the burden you're under and give you a renewed sense of purpose and ability.

Take inventory of what you're doing and what you really should be doing - often these are not the same. Keep the main thing the main thing and don't be afraid to say no. You can only do so much, and there's no shame in taking things off your plate. You are one person with a divine purpose, and anything not in alignment with this is not your assignment. Remember what you've been called to you.

Father, being a teacher is exhausting. It's a job that requires me to fulfill others' needs all day, and I often forget my own in the process. Remind me of your specific assignments in my life, and help me to say no to anything not in alignment with them. Remind me of the power of saying no to what isn't best for me and my students. Remind me that you offer rest that sleep won't bring, and you provide comfort in the midst of my storms. You are for me, and you will give me exactly what I need to do what you have called me to do.

Day 14 - It's Not About Me

"The heart of the wise makes his speech judicious and adds persuasiveness to his lips. Gracious words are like a honeycomb, sweetness to the soul and health to the body." Proverbs 16: 23-24

All over your building are people who work alongside you, but in a different capacity. There are administrators, counselors, janitors, and cafeteria workers. Their jobs are just as vital as yours, but often unappreciated, too. They perform tasks that are behind the scenes and unknown to the majority of the school. They don't work for applause, and they make difficult decisions that affect others.

Today, go out of your way to notice them and thank them. If you don't know them well, make an effort to strike up a conversation. Learn their names and what matters to them. Use your words graciously, since they are "sweet to the soul and healing to the bones." You, singlehandedly, can affect the climate of your school.

God, I become self-absorbed so easily. I only focus on what I am doing and how I am affected, but there are others around me who need a kind word. Help me notice them, God. Help me see their needs and listen to their voices. Reveal to me how I can help them, and let me use my words to uplift them. Remind me that this job and this life are not about me.

Day 15 - Learning What Makes Them Tick

"Fathers, do not provoke your children to anger, but bring them up in the discipline and instruction of the Lord." Ephesians 6:4

Those who don't work in education don't understand the relationship that forms between teachers and students. We spend hours and hours with these children, and after just a few weeks, we feel like we know them pretty well. Once you know someone well, it's inevitable that conflicts arise.

Ephesians 6:4 instructs us not to provoke children to anger. Again, when you know someone well, you know what pushes their buttons. As teachers we are tempted to feel the power we have been given. We have sole control over 30 (or more) people for several hours a day, and the natural temptation is to feel proud of being in control. Don't we all know a teacher who lives on a perpetual power trip? We can feel that power and demand that it's our way or no way. We know what causes our children anger, but we can easily feel that it's their job to conform to our expectations. We want everything done a certain way, and we don't always give our students a choice about the way. Is this not purposely provoking children to anger?

Think about the last time a child became angry or upset with you. Try to be objective and see where you had a role in that anger. What could you have done differently? How could you have treated the child with more understanding?

Today, determine that you will do everything in your power to keep your classroom a place of peace. Learn what makes your students tick and then avoid those things. Use your power for good and to uplift.

Father, humble me today. Yes, I have great power in my classroom, but I know that power comes with great responsibility. Help me understand that my children are not pawns in the game of school but are individual people you have trusted me to train. Give me insight into what each child needs from me and what each child needs me NOT to do and say. Fill me with your love, and let that love overflow to them.

Day 16 - More Than What Vision Reveals

"But the Lord said to Samuel, "Do not look on his appearance or on the height of his stature, because I have rejected him. For the Lord sees not as man sees: man looks on the outward appearance, but the Lord looks on the heart." 1 Samuel 16:7

In your classroom today, you will see a representation of the world in which you live. There will be rich students and poor, well-dressed and unbathed, confident and timid.

You will see students who look like they spent all morning on their hair, and you will see those who look like they've never brushed it. You will see designer clothes and hand-me-downs. Your human eyes will see the physical appearances, and your human tendency will be to place judgment on the child based on what you see.

But each child is so much more than what your vision reveals. The outward appearance is a disguise, a shell, hiding the true child. Inside and behind that facade is a complex person with needs and dreams and hurts you may never know. Even with people we love, we often mask our true selves. How much more will a vulnerable child hide from those in power over them?

Don't allow yourself today to play favorites or make assumptions based on what you see. Each child was created in the image of God, and each child deserves to feel the love of God. You be the one to share it.

Father, blind my eyes to what I see and open my heart to what you know. Help me to see each child in my room as a precious and unique being you have entrusted to my care. Prevent my heart from judgment and fill my room with your love.

Day 17 - Negativity Breeds Negativity

"For by the grace given to me I say to everyone among you not to think of himself more highly than he ought to think, but to think with sober judgment, each according to the measure of faith that God has assigned." Romans 12:3

Walking into the teacher's lounge can sometimes be like walking into a hornet's nest. As soon as I opened the door and heard her very loud and very public grumbling, I cringed. She was known around the building for her less than positive attitude, and this day's rant was evidence supporting everyone's judgment of her. She was negative. She hated the kids, she hated the administration, and by all appearances, she hated her job.

I tried to avoid being around her because I know negativity breeds negativity. This day, there was no avoiding it. As I listened to her complaints, I kept thinking things like, "Boy, I bet her students despise her. How demoralizing it must be to spend 90 minutes a day with her. I may not be the best, but at least I'm not like that."

I was judging her, yes, and I was thinking of all the reasons I was better than she was. I was taking the little I knew of her and was condemning her while puffing myself up. She may not have been right in her behavior, but neither was I. In fact, I was very wrong.

Scripture very clearly tells us to be honest in evaluating ourselves, and I failed that day.

It may be tempting to look at the teachers around you and see all the ways they fall short. Their bulletin boards may be shabby, their students may be rowdy, and their papers may not be returned on time. But never forget that you don't know what's going on behind the scenes of their lives, and never forget that the plank in your own eye is needing attention, too. Teaching is hard enough with us turning on each other. You can help to create an environment of positivity and support in your building. Decide to begin today.

Lord, I confess my judgmental spirit. I naturally want to see and celebrate everyone else's failures so I can feel I'm succeeding. How wrong I am. Let me be the one to celebrate my colleagues. Let me be the one to influence my school in positive ways. Let me be honest in looking at myself. Soften my heart, Lord, and make it more like yours.

Day 18 - Renewed in His Presence

"The steadfast love of the Lord never ceases; his mercies never come to an end; they are new every morning: great is your faithfulness." Lamentations 3:22-23

Teachers make mistakes. We don't want to, but we do, and though our mess-ups might be completely unintentional, they have consequences.

Most of us in this profession are detail oriented, perhaps even perfectionists, and we don't like to be wrong. When we are, we beat ourselves up and do everything we can not to repeat our mistakes. We demand excellence from ourselves just as much as we do from our students.

Here's the good news: yesterday's failures don't prevent today's successes. Every morning, we get a clean slate. Every day, we get another chance. Every time we wake up, the love and mercy of the Lord flood our lives and we are renewed in His presence.

What do you need to forgive yourself for doing? Saying? Where do you look back and see failure or disappointment in yourself?

The very thing that brings you shame and makes you feel condemnation can be released to the Lord, and you can live in the freedom that today is a brand new day.

God, how grateful we are that every morning, you give us a second chance. You never grow tired of our missteps and careless ways, and you never condemn us for wrong choices or lapses in judgment. You forgive and redeem, and you invite us to learn from you. We want desperately to be people who live in your mercy.

Day 19 - The Good in What He Allows

"Give thanks in all circumstances; for this is the will of God in Christ Jesus for you."
1 Thessalonians 5:18

A teenage girl I had never seen before stopped at my classroom door, holding a schedule in her hand. "I'm your new student," she said, thrusting the paper towards me. The look on her face told me she was less than happy to be there. (A schedule change in the middle of the semester is rarely a good thing when you teach high school.)

It was thirty seconds before the tardy bell. I had no extra desks and no extra handouts and no advanced warning that my classroom dynamic was about to change. It's not that I was unhappy she was there or unwilling to welcome her, but I was unprepared. And as a teacher, being unprepared is like throwing yourself to the wolves.

When the Bible says to be thankful in everything, that includes the interruptions, the unexpected, and even the unwanted. In all circumstances, there is a gift. That day, standing at my classroom door, I wasn't looking at the circumstance as a gift. I was only seeing the inconvenience. I was only feeling the frustration.

As I got to know my new student, I learned that she was a blessing to our class. Her presence changed the dynamic, yes, but it was a welcome and needed change. The interruption I had resented was a blessing in disguise.

Daily, you will be faced with circumstances you deem less than ideal. You will not always feel thankful, but you can always choose to be thankful.

Lord, forgive me for the times I have chosen to honor the natural emotions that well up in me rather than to honor your commandments for me. I confess that I see the inconveniences before I give thanks, and I grumble and complain before I offer praise. Change my heart, Lord, and let me see the good in all that you allow.

Day 20 - The Inevitability of Hard Times

"Then Jesus said, 'Come to me, all who labor and are heavy laden, and I will give you rest.'" Matthew 11:28

There's no worse time of the year for English teachers than research paper time.

They're a necessary evil, with evil being the key word. Teaching the research process to students who have always known Google feels like an exercise in futility. Worse than teaching the process, though, is grading the product. Reading, evaluating, and returning 75 papers in a timely manner can make even the most experienced teacher want to hide her head in the sand.

Regardless of what or whom you teach, there's a time of the year that's hardest for you, too. There's a unit you stumble through, a season that tries your patience, or a concept you just struggle to explain. The task is a burden, and you become weary. You seriously question if you can continue, and you wonder if this will be the time you fail miserably.

These hard times are inevitable, and they will not go away with years of experience or the best professional development. Trying times are a part of our business, and though they are burdensome and sometimes defeating, they are also necessary. They make you a better teacher. They cause you to question your methods, and they force you to self-evaluate. As in all of life, hard times make you better.

Lord, I feel like I lack what is required. I'm afraid I can't do this job well, and I want so desperately to be a teacher who makes a difference. The load I carry feels overwhelming at times, and the tasks seem beyond my reach. I'm tired, God, and I need your help. Give me the energy to continue moving, and give me the wisdom to know what's best.

Day 21 - The Marathon of the Classroom

"Therefore, since we are surrounded by so great a cloud of witnesses, let us also lay aside every weight, and sin which clings so closely, and let us run with endurance the race that is set before us."
Hebrews 12:1

Running a marathon sounded like a great idea when I signed up for it. It was on my bucket list, so I began training to run 26.2 miles.
When I started out, 3 miles was as far as I could go, so the idea of 26.2 seemed insurmountable. But I trusted the training plan and added a little distance each time I went out. Soon I was running 12, then 15, then 20 miles at a time. I was ready for the race, and on a crisp November day, the work paid off and I officially became a marathoner.

You might have no desire to run a marathon. But each of us has a 'race' God has set before us. This is true in our personal lives, and this is true of us as teachers. Each year is a race, but sometimes so is each day. God has intentionally set each race before us, and it is no mistake. You might envy others' races and wish for yours to be over, but the race you're running has purpose for your life.

Rather than wishing for it to be over, ask God what He wants to teach you in it.

Lord, racing is hard work. I get so tired and run down, and I want to stop for a break. Some days, I even want to quit. In those times of desperation, I'm asking you for help. Remind me that the assignment came from you, and reveal to me the purpose for which I'm running. Allow me to glimpse the lessons I need to learn, and keep my heart open to trust you in the race.

Day 22 - The Words They Remember

"Death and life are in the power of the tongue, and those who love it will eat its fruits." Proverbs 18:21

I was in 4th grade. The man who had been brought in by my school to teach a science lesson that day didn't know me. He didn't know my name, but I will never forget his. That day, he spoke unkind words to me, and nearly 30 years later, I still feel the sting. I can close my eyes and crawl back into the skin of that insecure little girl. I can remember the weight that his words held, and I can feel the shame flush my face again.

Words have power.

We can all remember words that have hurt us, whether intentional or not. We know what it's like to be at the mercy of someone's words, but in the day to day busyness and hustle of running a classroom, we can easily forget the power that our words have over the students filling our rooms. With our words, we can build or tear down. We can empower or demean, and we can encourage or destroy.

Teachers say thousands of words every day, and the ones our students remember aren't always about the content we teach. They remember the personal conversations and the compliments. They remember the jokes and the put-downs. They remember long after we've forgotten.

Make the decision before your students walk in today that your words will be uplifting and encouraging. Decide in advance that your words will be tools, not weapons. Remember what it's like to be wounded with words.

Lord, set a guard over my mouth today. Help me to pause before I speak and to see each child as a recipient of the life and death of my tongue. Let all my words be pleasing to you and edifying to them. Remind me of the power that lies in my words.

Day 23 - Understanding the Seasons

"For everything there is a season, and a time for every matter under heaven: a time to be born, and a time to die; a time to plant, and a time to pluck up what is planted; a time to kill, and a time to heal; a time to break down, and a time to build up; a time to weep, and a time to laugh; a time to mourn, and a time to dance; a time to cast away stones, and a time to gather stones together; a time to embrace, and a time to refrain from embracing; a time to seek, and a time to lose; a time to keep, and a time to cast away; a time to tear, and a time to sew; a time to keep silence, and a time to speak; a time to love, and a time to hate; a time for war, and a time for peace."
Ecclesiastes 3: 1-8

Being a classroom teacher is an exercise in understanding seasons. Through the course of one school year, you travel with students from blazing hot summer days to days filled with snow. But the seasons outside pale in comparison to the other seasons you face. During your time with these students, there will be times "for every activity under heaven."

Some days will be days of laughter and fun, interactive experiments and socializing. Other days will be full of standardized tests and stress, assessments and pressure. Some days you will be confident you are planting seeds that will lead to great harvests, and some days you will question whether you are planting anything that takes root.

The key is to remember that seasons come, but they also go. When you are stuck in a day (or week) that seems unending and frustrating, remind yourself that nothing is permanent in a school building. When you go home wanting to cry because your day seemed like an abysmal failure, remember that tomorrow the laughter will come back. Each day is a clean slate and brings a fresh start. For everything, there is a season.

Father, it's so tempting sometimes to believe the way I feel now is how I'll always feel. It's so easy to believe the way things are now is how they'll always be. But your word says otherwise, that seasons come and go. My task in the midst of them is to look to You and the lessons you want to teach me in them. Just as I walk my students through the changes they face, I trust you to walk me through my own.

Day 24 - We Are Acting on Behalf of God

"As each has received a gift, use it to serve one another, as good stewards of God's varied grace: whoever speaks, as one who speaks oracles of God; whoever serves, as one who serves by the strength that God supplies—in order that in everything God may be glorified through Jesus Christ. To him belong glory and dominion forever and ever. Amen." 1 Peter 4: 10-11

The ability to teach is a gift directly from God. Sometimes in the midst of trying days, when difficult students test our patience, we lose sight of the gift we have been given. We forget that the chance to impact children in our classroom is an enormous responsibility and a chance to glorify God. We are called to be "faithful stewards" of our skills in teaching.

What does it mean to be a faithful steward? It means to remember we are acting on behalf of God. We are to represent him through the gift of education, pointing children back to Him.

It means to act responsibly with those sitting under our teaching, handling them in the same manner Christ would. It means to remember we will one day give account to God for how we managed our gift. Nothing done in our classrooms or to our students will go unnoticed. Finally, it means that at some point we will be rewarded for our use of the gift in service to God.

The job you do every day is thankless and difficult, but at its core, it is a gift from the Father to you. It is a responsibility He has entrusted to you, and it is a way to give glory to the One who saved you.

God, thank you for the reminder that you have chosen me to do this. You have specifically gifted me to be an effective teacher, and you have provided the exact skills I need. My prayer today is that I will faithfully steward this gift. Everything I do is for your glory. Remind me of this when days get difficult. It is a gift, and it is for your glory.

Day 25 - We Teach Them How to Navigate the World

"Show yourself in all respects to be a model of good works, and in your teaching show integrity, dignity, and sound speech that cannot be condemned, so that an opponent may be put to shame, having nothing evil to say about us." Titus 2: 7-8

You may have a classroom full of tiny kindergarteners, or you may look out and see fully grown young adults. Regardless of their size or age, you have people every day who are looking to you. They are looking to you for answers and an education, yes, but they are also looking to you for what it means to be an adult. They are watching your example, and they are internalizing your treatment of them and the world. Your actions on a daily basis are teaching young people how to navigate their world.

Scripture encourages us to "be a model of good works." Many of the children watching you will be amazed by seeing good, because on a daily basis they are only exposed to very bad. Some of them have only seen inappropriate reactions to anger and a lack of self-control in what is said. They don't know how to handle their emotions, and they don't know what to do when they are sad.

You, for better or worse, are an example to your students. Determine before the day begins what example you'd like to be. Decide before a situation escalates how you will react. In all things, pray for the wisdom to do what is good, because little eyes are watching, learning, and becoming what you model.

Father, what an opportunity I have. On a daily basis, my actions can influence individuals and therefore the world for better. Through my words and behavior, I can teach a child the appropriate way to handle his feelings and the right ways to verbalize his thoughts. Let me never take this opportunity for granted, and let me never succumb to the temptation to react from a place other than love. Fill me with your Spirit, God, so it will flow out before my students.

Day 26 - What I Need and What I Want

"Count it all joy, my brothers, when you meet trials of various kinds, for you know that the testing of your faith produces steadfastness. And let steadfastness have its full effect, that you may be perfect and complete, lacking in nothing."
James 1:2-4

It's never good news when another teacher warns you that you have one of her former students.

When the teacher from down the hall came to me before classes ever began and started relating her horror stories with this particular young man, I cringed. I hate hearing about my students before I ever meet them, either good or bad. I avoid looking at test scores and permanent records before meeting the children because I want to know the human before I know the troubles.

But this teacher didn't mind coloring my perspective. He was awful, she said. Disruptive and disobedient. Lazy and a troublemaker.

Great, I thought. Here we go.

The first few days of class, he definitely tried to test me. He pushed his limits to see where they were, and I made it very clear when he crossed the line. He tried to be disruptive and disobedient, but I gave him not one inch. He tried to be lazy and a troublemaker, but I made it clear that wasn't an option. He pushed and tested, tried and tried. But I didn't give in. And when I didn't give in, he finally did. He finally accepted what the boundaries were in my room, and once he did, we had no horror stories. He wasn't a terrible student, as I had been told. He was just a student in need of clear parameters.

He tested me those first few weeks, but the trials he put me through changed me for the better. I became more resolute in what I would and would not allow, and I became more confident in myself as a classroom manager. It wasn't necessarily a joy to go through the tests, but the benefits were worth it all.

You will be tested. You will face hardships. You will struggle and wonder if it's worth it sometimes. The answer is always yes. You will be a better teacher, and your classroom will have a better environment if you persevere.

God, some days it's so hard to go through the trials I face. I want to avoid and escape them, but I know you have a plan in them. Give me the courage and tenacity to keep moving forward. Your word says that the testing of my faith produces steadfastness. Even though tests aren't my desire, I do want to be steady in my trusting of You, so bring what I need even if it isn't what I want.

Day 27 - What It's Like to Be Loved

"Love is patient and kind; love does not envy or boast; it is not arrogant or rude. It does not insist on its own way; it is not irritable or resentful; it does not rejoice at wrongdoing, but rejoices with the truth. Love bears all things, believes all things, hopes all things, endures all things. Love never ends. As for prophecies, they will pass away; as for tongues, they will cease; as for knowledge, it will pass away." 1 Corinthians 13: 4-8

Students who never feel safe, loved, or wanted at home walk through the doors of your school every day. Some of them may even walk into your classroom. Students who are physically hungry, emotionally starved, and spiritually anemic come to school looking for help. They may never voice it, but they need love. They may ask in unexpected ways, but they need you.

There is no greater gift you can give your students than love. If you have ever studied love languages, though, you know that everyone receives love in different ways. You may naturally be a hugger, but that doesn't mean every child needs a hug. Make it a point to learn how your students respond, and act accordingly. Pay attention to what makes them smile. Repeat it. Watch for what brings them into the group. Do it again. Ask them what makes them feel special. Go out of your way to act on it.

Remember that the standards you teach mean nothing if your students don't learn what it's like to be loved. You may be the only person in their lives to teach them this lesson.

God, I take for granted what it's like to be an adult who feels secure. Break my heart for the broken hearts of my students, and help me to play a role in their healing. Move me from my comfort zone so that I can be the hands and feet of Jesus in my classroom. When my students hear my name years from now, let them think, "That teacher loved me."

Day 28 - What to Do When You Need Guidance

"For to us a child is born, to us a son is given; and the government shall be upon his shoulder, and his name shall be called Wonderful Counselor, Mighty God, Everlasting Father, Prince of Peace."
Isaiah 9:6

When you read these verses, did you immediately think of Christmas? These verses have become as much a part of Christmas traditions as the gospel accounts, so we hear them in December, but often not during the rest of the year. Within them, though, is such beautiful truth about who our God is. He is our "Wonderful Counselor."

We all know what it's like to need someone to talk to, someone who will truly listen and then give us direction for our next steps. Those who are trained to give guidance can open us up to paths we've never considered, realities we've not acknowledged, and changes we've not been willing to make.

We teachers need good counselors, don't we? So often there are situations with our students that leave us at a loss. We don't know what to do, what to say, how to proceed. Education is about so much more than educating, and teachers know this better than anyone. We need guidance in what's best for our students, and since we're so involved with them on a daily basis, it can be hard to step back and see what's really needed. There is no better person to counsel us than the Creator. Not only did he create us and know how we work, but he also created the very students we need help with. He sees into the depths of who they are and knows with no limitations the situations they face. He will not always reveal these details to us, their teachers, but he will reveal what our responses need to be. He will counsel us on the approaches we need to take.

Our students are complex human beings, and we cannot adopt a "one size fits all" mentality with them. We need to differentiate their instruction, of course, but we also need to differentiate our interactions. Jesus is the Counselor who can lead us in these relationships.

Lord, let us never forget that when we are struggling to understand the complicated needs of our students, you alone have the answers. You will guide us in the choices we must make and show us the hidden things that need to be revealed. Let us never forget to ask you for counsel. We need it most of all.

Day 29 - What We Accept and What We Condone

"Train up a child in the way he should go: and when he is old, he will not depart from it." Proverbs 22:6

We like to think that our students' parents are responsible for training their children, and while they absolutely are, we cannot ignore the role we play in training them, too. For every child who sits in our rooms, we make an impact. We teach them what is acceptable and what is not, and we show them how to react by the choices we make ourselves.

We have a daily decision to make about the type of training we will give. We can train our students in self-control, tenacity, responsibility, and kindness, or we can train them in short-tempers, words spoken in anger, laziness, and excuses. What we accept is what we condone, and what we condone is what they are trained to repeat.

What are you training your children in? What changes do you need to make immediately in the environment of your classroom? What children learn is what they will do long-term. What are they learning from you?

God, thank you for teaching me that I'm teaching more than academics. Thank you for reminding me that I have a great role to play in molding my students' lives. As I go about each day, whisper to me when I need to make adjustments. Steer me in the directions I should go, and when I fall short, lovingly correct me. What I teach my students now will impact them for years to come. Let me never forget this.

Day 30 - When Truths Come to Light

"If any of you lacks wisdom, let him ask God, who gives generously to all without reproach, and it will be given him." James 1:5

She sat in the back corner of the room, long dark hair shielding her face. She rarely spoke, rarely smiled, rarely interacted with anyone. Although her grades were always high, I knew she was struggling. I just didn't know how.

It's uncomfortable sometimes to ask people what's wrong. We want to enter into their pain, but we don't want to make it worse. We want to acknowledge their hurt, but we don't want to publicize it. With our students, we want to make it better, but many times we can't.

I eventually learned that her parents were splitting up. She confided in me only after an assignment was left at the house she wouldn't see until the weekend, and she was afraid I'd be mad.

We sat down after school and talked, and I shared my own divorce experience with her. I walked her through my grief, and we shared a few small tears. I didn't know exactly what to say, but I wanted her to know I cared. Our conversation didn't cure her pain or change all tears to smiles, but it brought her experience into the open where light could shine into her darkness.

The truths that teachers learn about their students are often heartbreaking. We learn of hunger, abuse, self-harm, and unkindness. We hear of circumstances we never could have imagined and often have a hard time believing. When these truths come to light, we are often at a loss. We don't know what to say and what to leave unsaid, and we don't know what to do.

In these times, the best first step is to ask for wisdom from the wisdom-giver. We can make a mess when we step out in our own wisdom, deciding for ourselves what is best. Instead of jumping right in or being paralyzed by our fear, we need to ask for discernment and wisdom from the Lord. His word promises He will give it.

Father, our students look to us as sources of knowledge and people of wisdom, but so often we just don't know the steps we should take. When it comes to our students, we need your thoughts to determine our paths. Shine your light into the darkest places, and give us eyes to see how we can shine your light, too.

Made in the USA
San Bernardino, CA
12 November 2019